The Life of

Ernest Craddock

of Sheffield

J.P. Craddock

Published by John Peter Craddock

John Peter Craddock has asserted his right under the Copyright, Designs and Patents Act 1988 to be identified as the author of this work.

ISBN: 978-0-9516194-2-1

Contents

Acknowledgements

I would like to thank the following for their assistance with producing this book:
Peter Craddock, Philip Craddock, Anne Hodgson, Susan Mayock,
Elizabeth Wade & Philip Wadner.

-   and the staff of the following institutions –
The British Library; The Guildhall Library, London; The National Archives;
Sheffield Archives; Local Studies, Sheffield Central Library;
Society of Genealogists & Stevenage Central Library.

Introduction

In 1992 I proposed to research and write a biography of my grandfather Ernest Craddock. To that end, I hoped that my uncle, Stanley Craddock, would be willing to assist me but, being a retired deputy headmaster who had taught history and English at several Sheffield secondary schools, I was not too surprised when he told me he had decided to tackle the job himself. I was quite content with that at the time because I considered him to be the best person to do the job.

My uncle completed his privately produced book in 1994 which he subtitled 'A Short Biography'. I would never have dared suggest to him that a better subtitle would have been 'A Personal History' since a great deal of my uncle's character is contained within its 148 pages. Also, as he himself acknowledged, the account of his father's Great War army service is disproportionately long. My uncle had served in the Second World War, initially in the same unit, and his father's earlier service particularly fascinated him. Due to my uncle's comprehensive account, it was a challenging task to tailor the chapter of my grandfather's Great War service for this book. Personally, I consider his coal dealing business to be of greater interest.

Coal merchants, once so vital to everyone, have now virtually disappeared and details of the running of such concerns are generally missing from the literature and archives.

Occasionally I try to imagine the scene, the year before my birth, when my grandfather sold his business. Ledgers, dating back to his father-in-law's coal dealership early in the twentieth century, would have been handed over to the new owner. Only the current volumes would have been of use so the earlier ones would have been stored away until someone got around to disposing of them. It is usually futile to search for family history holy grails. The best approach is to construct the story from what is known and very often indications for further research may then become apparent.

I have made four major departures from my uncle's account of his father's life.

Firstly, I am sure that my grandfather was as curious as are many people about their family histories. Any reticence on his part was probably due to a short-lived rift with his father and he didn't want to dwell on that period in his later life. Unfortunately, that resulted in a distinct lack of information concerning his father's working life during his long career on the Midland Railway.

Secondly, my uncle was a great enthusiast for first-hand accounts. He liked to tell me, 'That man was there so he knew what happened'. However, that was not always the case and history can always benefit from hindsight, drawing from many sources and being viewed from a different perspective. My uncle had the view that there is a definitive and 'correct' account of history. In fact very little is set in concrete and much is open to interpretation. Having said that, history should always be set in the context of the time.

Thirdly, I have been able to draw upon family correspondence when my uncle was on active service during the Second World War and from that during my father's post-war National Service. A list of the above and other family correspondence indicates what a remarkable archive has survived and I have incorporated much of that and also information contained within my grandfather's Great War diaries into my account.

Finally, my uncle enjoyed horse-riding and held the view that if only the cavalry in the Great War could have amassed at the right time and the right place and with favourable conditions a breakthrough could have been forced.

Generals have always looked to the preceding war for guidance and in the case of the Great War it was that fought in southern Africa fifteen years earlier. That conflict relied on equine mobility over vast distances and was much removed from a European war of barbed wire, machine guns, no-man's land and hundreds of miles of trenches.

My grandfather enjoyed his activities with the Yorkshire Dragoons at the Scarborough camp at Whitsuntide 1914. At the time he, his fellow troopers and their officers would have sincerely believed that they were making valuable preparations for war. Unfortunately, subsequent events put paid to that. To put it plainly, other than being used as a beast of burden, the Great War made it quite clear that there was no place for the horse in modern warfare.

My uncle stated in his book that he was writing over a century after his father's birth and a quarter of a century after his death. More than another quarter century has passed by, and it is time for me to present my history of Ernest Craddock. I take full responsibility for any errors or omissions.

John Craddock   johncraddock17@yahoo.co.uk
9 Plash Drive, Stevenage SG1 1LW
October 2022

CHAPTER ONE

Hunsley Street

Ernest Craddock was born at 65 Hunsley Street in the Pitsmoor district of Sheffield on 17th July 1892, the youngest child of Joseph and Catherine ('Kate' née Howell). Ernest had older sisters, Edith aged eight and Nellie who was nearly three. He should have had two more siblings, Joseph Henry and Ethel, but sadly they died during their infancy before Ernest's birth.

Joseph Craddock, an engine driver on the Midland Railway, was forty-five when Ernest entered the world. A sad consequence of gaining that pinnacle of working class endeavour was that it gave him little time for family life. Ernest's early years were mainly spent in the company of his mother and his sisters. His mother's sister, Tilly Merrick, and her family lived nearly opposite the chapel at 49 Hunsley Street. Tilly's husband, Tom, was a fireman on the Midland Railway and a close friend and colleague of Ernest's father.

Ernest's maternal grandfather was killed in tragic circumstances in Sheffield in 1864. His widow remarried five years later and died the year before Ernest was born.

Ernest's paternal grandmother, Sabina Craddock, lived in Kettering in Northamptonshire. Whilst his father occasionally visited Kettering during the course of his railway duties, it appears that neither Ernest nor his sisters ever met their grandmother. The likely reason was that his father did not wish to emphasize the circumstances surrounding his illegitimacy and his early life in Kettering Union workhouse. In her poor old age Miss Sabina Craddock returned to that institution where she died in 1904 at the advanced age, for the time, of eighty.

Despite his deficiency in grandparents, Ernest had twenty-nine first cousins though four failed to survive infancy. They numbered fourteen with the surname Milner who were brought up in Darley in Derbyshire and two with the surname Kennedy in Kettering on his father's side of the family and seven Copnell, four Cripps and two Merrick on his mother's side in Sheffield.

Ernest enjoyed a life-long friendship with his cousin Ted Milner of Two Dales near Matlock. Ted's parents met, married and started their family in Kettering prior to employment on the Midland Railway taking them back to the Milner's home county of Derbyshire. Ted's older brother, Harry, joined the Grenadier Guards in 1896 and saw action at the Battle of Omdurman in the Sudan and, later, in the Boer War in southern Africa.

Ernest's Kennedy cousins emigrated to Australia in 1911 and 1912. He kept in touch with Arthur John Kennedy who joined the Australian Imperial Expeditionary Force and gallantly returned to Europe to fight for the British Empire during the Great War. The only subsequent contacts with that branch of the family occurred in 1921 when Arthur's sister-in-law visited Sheffield and in 1999 when Arthur's granddaughter and her husband joined a family gathering, also in Sheffield.

The Copnell family lived in Botham Street where Ernest's Aunt Polly had to work hard since, according to her niece Olive French, she had an idle husband. The couple's oldest child, George Thomas Copnell, was a professional footballer during the winter but his illegal street betting probably alienated him, and possibly other members of his family, from his aunts' families. However, Ernest kept in touch with his youngest Copnell cousin, Corporal Joseph Copnell, who emigrated to Canada and served in the Western Ontario Regiment during the Great War. Tragically he was killed in August 1918.

Another of Ernest's cousins, Charles Henry Cripps, was an engine cleaner on the Midland Railway but on a couple of occasions was caught idling in the mess room when he should have been at work. After leaving the railway, Charlie saw service in the Royal Flying Corps and then the Royal Air Force during the Great War. That appeared to put him back on track as he was promoted to sergeant and, after the war, he became a school caretaker. Charlie's half-sister, and Ernest's youngest cousin, Olive French, who died in 1999 at the age of ninety-five, was a fount of family knowledge.

The Unwin family lived at 52 Hunsley Street. The youngest of a brood of nine, Bert, was to become Ernest's brother-in-law.

As soon as he was allowed to venture out on Hunsley Street, Ernest befriended Harry Alvey who was born at no. 50 in February 1893 and whose father was also a driver on the Midland Railway. One of the youngsters' activities was cherry-bobs. That involved propelling a cherry stone up a rainwater down-pipe to see how far it would return and bounce across the pavement.

Ernest and Harry started Sunday School together at the Methodist Hunsley Street chapel. However, Ernest also attended All Saints Church of England Sunday School with his sister Nellie because their father went there when his railway duties allowed. Being aware that they should have had another older sister, the siblings fantasised about airborne dandelion seeds that they called angels and wondered whether one of them could be their Ethel.

Ernest and Harry entered Grimesthorpe Council School on Earl Marshal Road together and were placed in the same class. On 25th March 1898 the Sheffield School Board presented Ernest with Alma Strettell's book 'Lullabies of Many Lands' as a reward for punctual attendance. In 1900 Ernest received 'Yule-Tide Yarns' by G.A. Henty, as a first class reward also for punctual attendance. Ernest enjoyed reading and his nephew, Howard Robinson, recalled reading his uncle's copy of 'The Last of the Mohicans'.

The 1901 census indicates that a thirty-year-old railway fireman then lodged with the family. The most likely explanation is that Ernest's father had agreed to temporarily accommodate a colleague rather than for any need to supplement the household income. Unfortunately, that arrangement meant that nine-year-old Ernest had to share his attic bedroom for a time.

A benefit of employment on the railway was that free rail passes were available to employees and their families. On the strength of that, Joseph occasionally took his family for trips across the Midland Railway network and on at least one occasion, all the way to Bournemouth.

Joseph Craddock filed his last will and testament in 1903 and thus became the first of his family to do so. The document stipulated that his watch, presumably the one that he used on the railway, and chain were to go to Ernest upon him attaining sixteen years of age. It is not known what became of the watch but the gold chain and an ornament called an Albert, fashioned from a painted shilling, passed to Ernest's younger son.

In December 1903 W.H. Robinson, Ernest's future brother-in-law, joined the staff of Grimesthorpe Council School. At the same school, in March 1904, Ernest and three other boys were presented with prizes for their participation in the Sheffield Children's Hyacinth Show.

Later that year Ernest and Harry started at Owler Lane Council School on Owler Lane. Two years later he received a certificate for passes in reading, handwriting, spelling, composition and arithmetic. His work in geography, history, English and mechanics was deemed to be satisfactory. At around that time Ernest bought three identical Sheffield *Star* newspapers for a penny. He quickly sold two to break even but became a little concerned when the third was slow to sell.

Possessing an independent spirit and an entrepreneurial zeal, when Ernest left school in 1906 he found himself a job with James Willis Nicholson of Plumpton, Ecclesall, a partner of Francis Ebenezer Smith, a stocks and shares broker. For Ernest's father, who had greatly benefited from his career on the railway, trading in stocks and shares was beyond his experience and knowledge. As a consequence of that Ernest was compelled by his father to give up his job and secure a trade apprenticeship. Thus, he became an apprentice fitter at Vickers, Son & Maxim at the same time that Harry Alvey started work in the drawing office of nearby Charles Cammell's steel works.

Ernest and Harry continued their education at the Owler Lane Evening School and in July 1908 Harry gained first class and Ernest second class in the first year experimental mathematics course.

The earliest photographs of Ernest Craddock

Harry Alvey is fourth from the right in the back row
Ernest, second from the left in the front row

CHAPTER TWO

Earl Marshal Road

Although the denizens of the district around Hunsley Street formed a tight-knit community centred on the chapel for both worship and other means of social interaction, it was nevertheless a poor district of Sheffield.

After the Alvey family left Hunsley Street for Hamilton Road, Joseph Craddock decided to relocate his family to Earl Marshal Road. That road, which was then sparsely built upon and surrounded by fields, runs to the north of Pitsmoor between Crabtree and Grimesthorpe. Although it was open to public traffic, it was then a private road owned by the Duke of Norfolk's estate. To indicate that, a five-barred gate halfway along that had to be opened every time a vehicle passed by.

By means of his thrift and a mortgage from his trade union, ASLEF, Joseph had a pair of houses, nos. 405 and 407 Earl Marshal Road, built by Arthur Drew of Norwood Road. Upon completion, the Craddock family moved into 407 and 405 was rented to the Stone family for 18s per week. The head of the latter household, Richard Stone, had been a Midland engine driver under whom Joseph had once served as fireman.

In October 1908 Ernest's older sister, Edith, went to London during the final weeks of the Franco-British Exhibition at the White City. From there she sent a postcard to her sister Nellie at 65 Hunsley Street. From that, and other evidence, it appears that the move to Earl Marshal Road took place during the spring of 1909.

Unfortunately for Ernest, the sleeping arrangements in their new house remained unchanged; Edith and Nellie shared a bedroom, with Ernest in the attic. However, Ernest's lasting memory was the improvement in lighting provided by the gas mantles in comparison to the naked flame bats-wing burners at Hunsley Street.

Edith pursued a career in teaching and became more involved in the running of Hunsley Street chapel including playing the organ. Those activities brought her close to Willie Robinson, a fellow teacher and the chapel's financial secretary. In March 1909 a three-day bazaar was held at the chapel with the objective of raising the huge sum of £150. Ernest's mother and Edith helped tend the Ladies' Congregational Stall whilst Nellie was at the Crockery Stall. Ernest, Harry Alvey and others manned the Bazaar Room Entertainments.

On two occasions, Ernest and Harry Alvey, who were to become life-long friends, cycled to Wichenford to the north-east of Worcester to spend a fortnight with Harry's aunt. On the outward journey they called on Ernest's aunt, Susan Milner, and her family at Two Dales near Matlock. A faded photograph has been preserved of Ernest, Harry, Oswald Bunn and Tom Butterworth with their bicycles at Mortomley to the north of Sheffield. It is fascinating to appreciate that whilst they rode the fastest vehicles they were likely to encounter on the roads, Ernest's and Harry's fathers drove steam locomotives, then the fastest vehicles devised by man.

In later life Ernest recalled the time when the crowd at Bramall Lane would applaud skilful play at football as well as at cricket.

Whilst he enjoyed watching Yorkshire County Cricket Club in action, Ernest was just as keen to play the game himself. In June 1908 Ernest and Harry Alvey played for the Hunsley Street chapel team against Newhall Primitives at Blackburn Meadows. At the close of play Ernest was not out. In May 1909 he and Harry played for the same team against St. Clement's at Meadow Hall.

Harry was run out but Ernest was not out. Four years later, Ernest and Harry remained members of the team under the captaincy of H.O. Bunn with Tom Butterworth and Joseph Copnell, Ernest's cousin. Ernest was also secretary of the Hunsley Street chapel football team and he probably learned to play billiards at the same institution.

Edith Craddock and Willie Robinson were married on 29th May 1912 at Hunsley Street chapel. Nellie's young man, Bert Unwin, served as Willie's best man. After the ceremony a few guests were entertained at 407 Earl Marshal Road where the happy couple received gifts from family, friends and their respective schools and a photograph was taken to record the occasion. Due to the convention of the day, marriage also marked the end of Edith's teaching career.

Dancing lessons have always provided a good means for young people of the opposite sex to meet as Ernest discovered at Thomas Dey's Tower Ballroom on Pitsmoor Road. Teachers of dancing at that time used the title 'Professor'. Ernest recalled that his heels were chalked so that the error of allowing them to touch the floor during the waltz would be made apparent. One Friday night in 1913, he met sixteen-year-old May Rideout and her friend Lilah Telfer who had noticed 'the boy with the dreamy eyes'.

Victoria May Rideout was so named because she was born on the day that Queen Victoria visited Sheffield in her Diamond Jubilee year. May was the only surviving child of Henry Rideout, a coal merchant, and his wife Emily of 170 Scott Road in Pitsmoor. Ernest and May attended a ball at Dey's on a wet, snowy and slushy Saturday night and afterwards they visited the cinema.

Joseph Craddock's responsible and demanding job as an engine driver left little time for the usual father/son activities. Also, the forty-five year age gap and

Joseph's limited view of the world beyond that of the railway would have presented further obstacles.

Joseph's intervention in Ernest's early working life and perhaps other incidents probably initiated the latter's desire to strike out on his own having reached his majority. Thus, it appears that early in the new year of 1914 Ernest left 407 Earl Marshal Road without telling his parents his destination. The following appeared at the top of the front page personal column of the Sheffield edition of the *Yorkshire Telegraph & Star* on 16th February.

Craddock – Why keep away? Come home – Father and Mother

It is hoped that Ernest's parents did not have long to wait before they learned that he was safe and well. They would then have learned that he had joined 'A' Squadron of the Queen's Own Yorkshire Dragoons on 21st February.

At Vickers, Ernest had become acquainted with a fellow employee, Matt Sheppard, a veteran of the Territorial Force, which became known as the Territorial Army after the 1908 army reforms.

Born in 1873, Matt Sheppard joined the Imperial Yeomanry from the Queen's Own Yorkshire Dragoons in 1900 in which he saw active service against the Boers in South Africa. Early in the new century, Matt rejoined the Yorkshire Dragoons and, as he rose through the non-commissioned ranks, became a valuable recruiting sergeant for the regiment. Indeed in 1913 Matt was promoted to squadron sergeant-major, 'A' Squadron's senior non-commissioned officer.

For Ernest, the attraction of the Yorkshire Dragoons would have been the camaraderie associated with being a member of the regiment and an escape from his work and parental home. In February 1914 it was announced in the local press that the Whitsuntide annual training camp was to be at Scarborough and Ernest would have eagerly anticipated the event.

On 30th May, 'A' Squadron, Queen's Own Yorkshire Dragoons paraded outside the Great Central Railway station (later renamed the Victoria station) in Sheffield.

There they were inspected by Lieutenant Douglas C. Leng who was accompanied by Squadron Sergeant-Major Matt Sheppard. A photograph was taken of a group, which included 2765 Trooper Ernest Craddock, all looking happy to be heading for the seaside.

At the camp in Towend's field, the regiment of between 430 and 440 officers, NCOs and men, was under the command of Major W. McKenzie Smith (soon to be promoted lieutenant colonel). There they took part in a musketry course at Scalby Beck, mounted drill on Scarborough race course and field days in the countryside. One of the officers, Lt. Hon. E.F.L. Wood MP, the future Lord Halifax and Foreign Secretary, was promoted to captain during the changeable weather they experienced at that camp.

On 4th June the regiment was inspected by the Director-General of the Territorial Army and four days later by the General Officer Commanding the Northern Command. For generals and troopers alike the possibility of a major war in Europe two months later must have appeared to be quite remote. For his memorable fifteen days activity Ernest was awarded a one pound bounty and he arrived back home riding his horse!

Edith & Willie Robinson's wedding, 29th May 1912
Ernest is standing next to his sister Nellie
Edith is flanked by her parents
Bert Unwin is on the extreme right

Ernest & SSM Matt Sheppard amongst a group of 'A' Squadron QOYD, June 1914

CHAPTER THREE

The Great War

Although the Territorial Army was for home defence only, upon the outbreak of war, the drill hall at 93 Brunswick Street was besieged by men, including Ernest, who wished to volunteer for service overseas. Squadron Sergeant-Major Matt Sheppard tried to bring about order with his 'stentorian voice, eagle eye and merciless invective'. He was assisted in that task 'by the neat and polished yet none the less effective sarcasm' of the squadron commander, Major Philip G. Smith.

'A' Squadron, Queen's Own Yorkshire Dragoons was successfully embodied the following day, 5th August. The unit's strength was then 124 and the men were billeted for the night at various hostelries in the neighbourhood or in their own homes if close by. The next few days were very busy as they undertook tactical and skirmishing exercises.

The squadron then entrained for Doncaster where they slept on the race course grandstand prior to joining the rest of the regiment. They then embarked on a march to the east coast when a welcome break was made at Tadcaster where every man was provided with a pint of John Smith's best bitter from the brewery. Training began at Londesborough Park near Market Weighton where additional recruits brought the regiment up to strength. They then proceeded to positions between Scarborough and Spurn Head from where they hoped to impede a possible invasion. The regiment was equipped and trained for overseas service and, to that end, every man was asked to sign an Imperial War Service obligation. 'A' Squadron was billeted at farms around Grimston Hall until

January 1915 when Ernest used his leave to take May to a dance before returning to his parents' home at 407 Earl Marshal Road.

Ernest re-joined his unit at Hornsea where they practiced on the rifle range and in February they marched to Filey and then returned to Scarborough. Unfortunately, Ernest spent the last week of the month in bed with a 'dose of the flu'. When he finally received the doctor's permission to get up he would have been delighted to find a parcel from May.

In March, swords were distributed and sword drill conducted indicating that they were expected to perform as cavalry as well as mounted infantry. They were inspected by the honorary colonel of the regiment, the Earl of Scarbrough, conducted bayonet drill and practiced rifle shooting on the range. Midway through the month, Ernest had forty-eight hours leave to Sheffield when he took May to the Coliseum cinema and walked with his father, sister Nellie and Harry Alvey.

At Easter, Ernest met May at Scarborough railway station and took her to visit his friends the Linton couple where she stayed for the weekend. After returning to his duties, Ernest managed to spend the whole of 5th April with May before seeing her off at the station at 8pm.

In May and June the regiment spent three weeks at Pitt Corner Camp near Winchester re-equipping and conducting drill. In a post-script to a letter to May, Ernest asked her whether he should bring back a German helmet. Ernest subsequently acquired a pickelhaube but, after finding it a burden to carry around, retained only the badge.

On 1st July the regiment was inspected by Lt. Gen. Pilcher, then on 15th they marched to Southampton where they boarded HMT *Huanchaco* which docked at Le Havre the following day.

The regiment's first role on the continent was as divisional cavalry and, to that end, the squadrons were attached to different units. 'A' Squadron served with the 17th (Northern) Division, V Corps, 2nd Army. The squadron entrained for Lumbres, with men and horses accommodated in identical wagons. On his twenty-third birthday Ernest, in 4th Troop, marched to Esquerdes and re-joined the rest of the squadron two days later. All enjoyed the novelty of marching through the French countryside and Ernest wrote to May that it was amusing trying to talk to the locals.

On Saturday 24th July Ernest's thoughts were very much of Sheffield when his sister Nellie married Bert Unwin at Hunsley Street chapel. Ernest particularly regretted being unable to be present because May was one of the bridesmaids. Bert's best man was Percy Barrand who lodged with Ernest's parents at 407 Earl Marshal Road. Bert was tenant of the Robinsons at 101 Scott Road and after the nuptials he and Nellie set up home at 51 Idsworth Road.

Behind the vast system of trenches on the Western Front, the cavalry were kept in constant readiness waiting for a gap to be forced through into open country. Until that occurred the cavalry acted as mounted infantry, undertook observation work and formed trench working parties. Units were continually kept on the move and detachments formed to give the impression that progress was being made and to keep the men occupied.

On 6th August the then commissioned 2nd Lieutenant Matt Sheppard led 4th Troop on an exercise ride under shellfire. Ten days later the same officer led a sixteen man detachment, including Ernest, which had been seconded for duties at V Corps HQ at Abeile. After a few days of riding as orderlies to Major (later Colonel) Hill and Captain Thomas, Ernest rejoined the squadron at Boeschappe. From there the 17th Division moved behind the Ypres Salient where they endured the drenching autumnal weather.

In December Ernest had a week's leave in Sheffield when he spent most of his time with May and her parents and visiting the Robinsons before departing at 4am on 13th December. In Abeile, Ernest enjoyed good dinners to mark his first Christmas Eve and Christmas Day on the continent.

Ernest's duties with V Corps HQ ended in the New Year of 1916 when he re-joined 'A' Squadron.

During a morning ride with Matt Sheppard, Ernest learned that he had recommended him for a lance corporal's stripe. A week later, Ernest had a 'joy ride' with corporals Haynes and Williams as they looked for two lost mules.

Football was then a diversion; Ernest's team lost 8-0 to the Motor Machine Gun section and then 3-2 to the Cyclists. Then, whilst acting as postman for the week, his team won 13-3 with Ernest scoring a hat trick!

21st February, his second anniversary of joining the Yorkshire Dragoons, was significant enough for Ernest to make a note of it in his diary. Unfortunately, around that time he noticed that he was suffering from haemorrhoids, probably caused by damp saddles.

On 2nd March, under a terrible bombardment that lasted all day, Lieutenants Leng and Sheppard took forty men, including Troopers Craddock and Gilliat, up the trenches to escort German prisoners back to a cage. Ernest found an enemy map that he handed in to the office with the expectation that it would provide useful intelligence. On 19th March he acted as orderly to Matt Sheppard for the day and two days later he was promoted lance corporal.

Proudly displaying his stripe, Ernest was corporal of the guard for the night of 29th/30th March. During the latter day he noted in his diary that it was his nephew Howard Robinson's first birthday.

The St. George's Day church parade was followed by a ride to Armentieres and, the next day, machine gun drill guided by Matt Sheppard. On 26th April a few horses stampeded during afternoon exercise and Ernest's horse Lizzie was killed. The next day Ernest helped with the huge job of digging her grave.

On 30th April, Ernest and others in the squadron suffered sore throats after a German gas attack. Major P.G. Smith was eventually invalided home due to its effect.

On 10th May 'A' Squadron marched west to Hazebrouck to join the rest of the regiment under Lt. Col. W. Mackenzie Smith. They were then II Corps cavalry under Lt. Gen. Sir Claud Jacob. Ernest posted a present to his father for his birthday on 18th but a more significant entry in his diary was for May's birthday three days later. That day Ernest was signalling corporal for the squadron under Lieutenant Bates.

In mid June the squadron marched through the night towards the Somme. Then on 24th, the day after an inspection by General Jacob, Ernest recorded in his diary that a quarter of the squadron was poisoned by the bully beef at breakfast. Ernest was 'feeling rotten' by tea time as he and eighteen others went to hospital. The majority were discharged the next day including Ernest who left at 6-30pm 'feeling a bit seedy'. He then joined the sick parade for the remainder of the month.

On 1st July, the first day of the Somme offensive, Ernest became forage corporal for the week. Five days later he met up with members of the Sheffield City Battalion, including May's uncle Frank Rideout, which had suffered such appalling casualties. Later that month the regiment was in Senlis where they spent two days burying the dead. Ernest was with a party that found a dug-out containing several corpses. The only thing they could do was to collapse it.

With little prospect for mounted action, detachments were sent for corps duties. As a result of that, on 30th July, Ernest volunteered for duty with an observation troop that comprised three officers and thirty-six men under Capt. C.J. Hirst. After receiving instruction, in the course of his duties Ernest reported a German relief taking place. Since at that moment twice as many troops were in the same place, it made an ideal artillery target. In later life Ernest told his older son that he must have been partly responsible for dozens of deaths but then reflected that that was what had to be done at the time.

After enduring a wet October, Ernest was busy all day on 1st November as acting orderly corporal. Four days later, 'feeling rotten' he retired to bed for a week with flu. However, he was well enough on 11th to contribute to a 6-1 win at football. Ernest also had a 'good match' on 19th but, on 1st December, as they left Senlis by lorry, he was again 'feeling rotten'. The next day, after seeing the doctor, he was put on light duties for three days. However, he was soon up and about to compete in football matches including one on Christmas Day when his team lost 1-0 in a competition semi-final. On Boxing Day Ernest and three fellow NCOs were detailed to attend a course of instruction concerning the duties of linesmen with II Corps Signals.

In the extremely cold new year of 1917 Ernest helped to escort prisoners to Acheux. He judged the senior German present to be a 'very decent fellow'.

At the beginning of March he returned to the Squadron at Senlis, placed in charge of remounts and acquired for himself a fine brown mare. A few days later again 'feeling rotten', he saw the doctor and spent a day in bed.

A composite squadron was formed and ordered to reconnoitre the area in front of the 54th Brigade, 18th Division. After a night march and a two day sweep over the ground in pouring rain, no contact was made with the enemy. However, on 19th March, 'A' Squadron had an 'exciting scrap' with the enemy at St. Leger with only two men 'knocked out'. Having found the enemy occupying a wood they dismounted and cleared it with Hotchkiss and rifle fire. When British infantry took over their positions the Dragoons returned to Senlis. Unfortunately, Ernest's mare was lamed during the operation. Then on 31st March he received a second stripe on his promotion to full corporal.

Training and detachment duties occupied Ernest during April and May; including 4th Troop helping to staff the riding school near St. Omer. At the end of May Ernest set out for Sheffield where he spent most of his time with May, had tea at her house and with the Robinsons. After another tea and a visit to the Hippodrome cinema with the Rideouts, Ernest popped the question to May's father. In a letter, Ernest told May about the little talk he had had with her father at the gate. 'It was the ideal place to ask such a question, cool and dark and with plenty of room to run'. 'But no May, your father is fine and I shall make a real good friend of him.' On 8th June the couple went to town to buy a ring and later that same day Ernest returned to the Western Front.

After the joyous activities of the last few days it was perhaps not surprising that Ernest felt fed up back in camp at Sombre a few miles from Gris-Nez. However, the riding school and the regimental sports day helped to lift his spirits. Ernest and his friend Colin Dawes cycled to Calais in glorious weather that he described as 'ripping sport'. The following day the riding school was conducted on the sands in the morning and then they enjoyed their evening sea bathing. 'This is the life' he wrote in his diary. He wrote to May that the pleasant weather had made him a 'trifle dusky' and that her letters to him were 'such "rippers" and keep me going fine'.

That pleasant existence continued into July with racing, troop and squadron drill on the sands. On 8th July he and Colin cycled to Wimereux and took a tram to Boulogne. 'A' Squadron then spent six weeks escorting prisoners back from the trenches during which Ernest had a nasty fall with his horse.

September was spent looking after the horses and playing football. At the beginning of October the squadron was inspected by General Jacob and in November, after re-joining the regiment, they left II Corps for the 3rd Army. At the battle of Cambrai four hundred tanks helped to breach the Hindenberg Line and then the cavalry, including the Yorkshire Dragoons, moved to the bridges over the Canal d'Escourt but there was no breakthrough. The following month

Ernest was once again amongst working parties in the trenches. Then, on Boxing Day he found himself in Etaples on a Lewis Gun course.

In the new year of 1918 Ernest left for Amiens and had the good fortune to be put up at the Hotel du Rhin which was usually reserved for staff officers.

However, he was brought back down to earth when 4th Troop formed working parties in the trenches and had a spell as front line infantry. On 23rd January his party was spotted by 'Jerry' and they again made things uncomfortable. That activity extended into February when a night raid gave them a very busy time. Ernest spent all night on a fire step then a 'Boche' trench was raided; 'rather a risky business but things turned out ok'.

At the end of February the regiment was officially dismounted and in March mustered as a cyclist battalion attached to II Corps, 4th Army. 'A' Squadron was conveyed by lorry and train to Proven near Poperinghe from where they cycled ten miles to Road Camp at the base of the Ypres Salient. On 1st April Ernest moved up the line to reconnoitre battle positions. A week later he proceeded to the II Corps Lewis Gun School for a course of instruction in the company of 2nd Lieutenant W. Brock and Sergeant Siswick.

With the German spring offensive and Field Marshal Sir Douglas Haig's 'With our backs to the wall' speech, Ernest and others at the School were conveyed by lorry east to defend St. Jean Capelle, north of Balleul. Ernest wrote in his diary 'Very hot. Jerry busy', prior to helping guide in a relieving Australian battalion. The Yorkshire Dragoons marched around Mont des Cats several times to give the enemy observers an exaggerated impression of their strength.

In May, as Ernest suffered flu for a week, his thoughts would have been of his fiancé back in Sheffield. The day before May's twenty-first birthday, Ernest's older sister, Edith Robinson, wrote to commend her on her devotion to

Ernest and to tell her that she had never found him out in anything underhand or dishonourable.

At Ypres Ernest took a casualty to a field hospital before rejoining 4th Troop. Then, at the beginning of June, the Yorkshire Dragoons left Ypres bound for Houtkerque, six miles west of Poperinghe. Midway through the month Ernest acted as orderly sergeant for a day prior to the company cycling to Dunkirk.

Along with the majority of his comrades, Ernest could envisage no end to the situation and he just wanted to get out of the sludge and plant his feet on good firm pavement. That, along with the shortage of officers, initiated Ernest's application for an officer's commission.

When his application was unsuccessful, his commanding officer, Lt. Col. R. Thompson, realised that the probable reason was that Ernest had stated that his father was an engine driver. After an interval, the colonel sent him again with the instruction to say that his father was an engineer. On that occasion he was accepted.

Thus, on 8th July, Ernest commenced a probationary course with 112th Battery, 3rd Heavy Brigade, Royal Garrison Artillery. He was then attached to a 9.2 inch gun battery and engaged in action for ten weeks. At the end of August Ernest wrote to May that the war, if nothing else, had proved that their love for one another was the real thing. They could not have had a stronger test.

On 15th September Ernest walked through Ypres to the railhead and the next day he was back in Sheffield. Met at the station by May, Nellie and Bert, Ernest greatly enjoyed his fourteen day's leave. He then left, not to cross the English Channel once more but to 2 'B' Brigade, Royal Field Artillery Cadet School in Brighton.

In that seaside resort Ernest sat for written papers and learned that he had passed the maths exam prior to another week's leave in Sheffield. Back in Brighton, during the following couple of months he was occupied with parades and inspections and then learned the joyous news that the Armistice had been signed. All officer training ceased and Ernest could freely enjoy the attractions of the resort before a special train conveyed him back to Sheffield for Christmas.

On 3rd January 1919 Ernest returned to Brighton in very wet weather. There he saw young lads, barely out of school, being demobilised whilst he was kept busy on the parade ground and playing billiards.

Then, on 15th January Ernest travelled up the country to Ripon to receive his 'ticket'. Offered the choice of a suit or a pound sterling in cash, and having seen the suits, he opted for the cash. The next day he arrived back in Sheffield to recommence his civilian life.

For his service during the Great War Ernest received the 1915 Star, the British War and Victory medals.

May Rideout at 170 Scott Road

Trooper Ernest Craddock

CHAPTER FOUR

The Business

On 20th January 1919 Ernest went to Metropolitan-Vickers Electrical Manufacturing Company at the River Don works to see Mr. Campbell where it was agreed that he would recommence work the following Monday. Ernest noted in his diary that 'things seem very strange'. He was eased back in by being placed on repairs for a fortnight before returning to piece work.

At the beginning of February Ernest noted in his diary that he had paid his mother £2 and Nellie £6 presumably indicating that he also stayed with his sister and her husband Bert at 51 Idsworth Road. A month later he noted a 'very Mondayish day at Vickers'. The following day it was 'still feeling Mondayish'.

In contrast to his difficulty in adjusting to his new job and surroundings, Ernest's relationship with May went from strength to strength. On 12th March, when her parents went to the Hippodrome cinema, Ernest visited 170 Scott Road 'to look after the horses' belonging to Henry Rideout's coal dealing business.

From the end of July into August, Ernest and May enjoyed good weather at Bridlington for a fortnight's holiday. In accordance with the conventions of the day, they were almost certainly chaperoned by Nellie and Bert. Two days after returning to Sheffield, Ernest was back at work at Vickers. In June a drawing of a pedal car appeared in Ernest's diary and, with help from Bert, it was made in time for Christmas when they presented it to their nephew, five-year-old Howard Robinson.

Ernest and May were married at St. James' Presbyterian Church on Scott Road by the Rev. James Wallace on 2nd June 1920.

It is curious that Percy Barrard, the lodger at 407 Earl Marshal Road was Ernest's best man rather than Harry Alvey. Presumably their absence from the group photograph indicates that Harry and his wife Nora were then indisposed. However, Percy had been Bert's best man at his marriage to Nellie in 1915. May's friend, Laura Ward, was the matron of honour and her young cousins, Joyce Fletcher and Margaret Draper were the bridesmaids. Horse-drawn carriages conveyed the wedding party.

During the reception, which was held at Dey's Tower Ballroom, May's uncle, Arthur Rideout, who was a professional photographer, took a splendid photograph of the couple surrounded by a great gathering of members of their families. May's family outnumbered Ernest's by a fair margin and Percy Barrand, Laura Ward and her future husband Billy Bagshaw were the only non-family members present. The send off with decorations attached to the back of the taxi, was matched by that at the station as the couple were sent on their way to their honeymoon in Llandudno.

After the nuptials the couple spent three months with May's parents at 170 Scott Road before moving into one of the first council houses, 52 Edensor Road on the Norwood Estate.   It was there that Ernest and May's first child was born on 12th April 1921. The boy was christened Stanley Rideout Craddock in memory of May's brother, Stanley Hazell Rideout, who had died in infancy twenty years earlier.

When Stanley Craddock was three months old the family spent a pleasant fortnight in Southport as guests of May's widowed aunt Ada Hazell. Ada's husband, James Henry Hazell, had been a pawnbroker in Crookes in Sheffield but, when James suffered ill health and the couple retired to Southport where James died in 1917. When the Craddock family next visited Southport Ernest's working life had undergone a profound change.

In contrast to his personal life, Ernest found his working life at Vickers not so cordial. There was industrial unrest as men protested at the reduced wages of the immediate post war years. Some boasted of their wartime earnings when Ernest was on the continent fighting for king and country. Luckily, his marriage presented him with an alternative means of making a living.

Although he had only just turned fifty, Ernest's father-in-law, Henry Rideout, suffered from progressive paralysis that brought about his inability to manage his coal merchant business. His offer of a partnership to Ernest suited both men but May was not quite so keen since she remembered the occasions when she was asked to dash to the bank with cash so that a supplier's cheque could be honoured. She was certain that the money that Ernest could bring into the business was pretty much all there was. Nevertheless the partnership went ahead with Ernest as the mainstay from the start. Each working day he cycled the hilly mile from Edensor Road to Scott Road since there was no other form of conveyance.

Early in the century, when Henry Rideout wished to make a break from his father's coal dealing concern, he anticipated the custom that would be generated as Scott Road was developed. He had built a pair of houses that backed onto Burngreave Cemetery, nos. 168 and 170 Scott Road. His family were to live in 170 whilst 168 was let. Henry asked the builder, Walter Drew, to provide him with a stable to the rear of 168 that could be accessed from the driveway alongside 170. That is the reason why, to this day, no.168 has a short back garden.

Ernest commenced work with Tommy, the one remaining horse, but realising that the business needed to be modernised, horse, cart, dray and harness were advertised to be sold in November 1921. By then he had bought a Ford Model T one-ton lorry that was imported directly from the U.S.A. and so had a left-hand drive. It was fitted with a 30 cwt body and Ernest was so delighted with his purchase that he had photographs taken of himself and his father-in-law posing with the vehicle. Having had the controls described to him, Ernest would have learned to drive by trial and, hopefully, not too much error.

Despite the freedom associated with running the business, Ernest had embarked on a life of unremitting physical hard work.

Having received a note from the colliery supplier informing him that the coal he had ordered would be available on a particular date, Ernest, in leather coat and his cavalry riding breeches with leather leggings, would drive his employee mate to no. 8 Midland Railway (soon to become LMS) Coal Depot sidings off Savile Street. Having found his railway wagon, Ernest would draw the lorry alongside then, as his mate supported the door with his shoulders, he would knock-up the latches with an ash pole. The door would then be lowered as the coal spilled out onto the bed of the lorry and the ground. Then followed the laborious two-man job of shovelling the contents of the wagon into hundredweight bags and as each was filled it was lifted onto scales for weighing. Bags were then stacked on to the lorry bed.

Ernest was a precise man and his younger son remembered hearing of the occasion when the adjustment of the contents of a bag by adding or removing a lump of coal caused some amusement to fellow workers engaged in the same activity. The point was that Ernest was dealing with his own coal and he neither wanted to give coal away or supply his customers with a short measure. The other workers were no doubt employed by a large city firm and, consequently, were unconcerned by such niceties. On one occasion around 1925, when Sheffield's notorious gangs were active, Ernest stood his ground, shovel at the ready, to see off a pair of thugs intent on stealing his coal.

With the coal bagged and weighed it was then delivered to his customers. For the strenuous work of unloading and carrying hundredweight bags of coal

Ernest and his mate wore a leather protectors on their backs. Deliveries were usually made by tipping coal down a grate at the front or side of a house, directly into the coal cellar. Empty bags were carefully stacked so that he and the customer could check the quantity delivered. As Ernest drove around the district May would place an envelope in the front window as a signal for him to call in.

At home at the end of the working day, Ernest would entertain both himself, and any others within earshot, with baritone renditions of his favourite popular songs as he bathed. Then, having changed into a comfortable suit, the youngest of his children would sit on his knee and use their small fingers to remove any remaining specs of coal dust from the corners of his eyes. Ernest would then spend a portion of the evening writing out bills from his notebook and keeping the business accounts. He was constantly frustrated by professionals and others with a regular income who were slow to settle their bills.

When there were no collections or deliveries to be made, Ernest would do repairs. There were coal bags to be darned with a ball of twine using a large curved needle and the lorry bed to be reinforced. On one occasion a sheet steel advertising sign was used for that purpose. As a young boy, Howard Robinson would wander over from his home in Ellesmere Road and hang about the yard of no. 170 in the hope that his uncle would offer him a ride in his lorry. Howard later claimed that those occasions were the red-letter events of his early life.

In the winter Ernest would hang a coal fire from the lorry tailboard to thaw out both frozen bags and hands. He suffered from the arduous work and his hands became deeply cracked. After washing his hands using a sandy soft-soap compound, Ernest would rub in goose-grease for relief.

Ernest also used his lorry to develop a haulage side to the business.

Morton & Storer were mineral suppliers to steel and other works. Their manager, Charlie Bufton, provided a lot of work for Ernest transporting limestone from Derbyshire quarries and they became good friends.

At Whitsuntide several Sheffield churches joined together for the traditional march at Firth Park. Ernest's lorry was given a thorough spring-clean and, in the afternoon, used to transport people, equipment and food to the park for games and races.

During the General Strike of May 1926 when household coal was rationed to a hundredweight a fortnight, Ernest augmented his supplies from a non-union outcrop at Troway in Derbyshire.

In about 1927 the Ford lorry was superseded by a Dennis 30 cwt model to accommodate the growing haulage side of the business. Ernest drove the cab-less Dennis to Manchester where it was fitted with a cab and a two-ton body. Later the original solid tyres were replaced by pneumatics. With the help of the Hornbuckles, the monumental masons, whose yard was adjacent to the site, Ernest extended the garage he had built for the lorry in the yard behind 170 with materials purchased from the demolition of Coal Aston aerodrome. He used the old stable for his car (and another that was later abandoned there). Along the back wall of the yard a row of small garages was built, each of which could accommodate a small car or a motorcycle and sidecar. Those generated further income.

Ernest worked hard to support his family and parents-in-law and was not envious of those who were in a more fortunate situation. He appreciated that wealth could be earned more easily and found it difficult to accept that anyone could be worth a reported £30,000 a year; a huge income during the depression.

In about 1936 the Dennis was replaced by a Bedford three-ton lorry that was bought from Bentley Brothers' garage. It was painted maroon and 'E. Craddock' was emblazed in gold on the cab door. The tailboard declared that

'The Best is the Cheapest'. Ernest was tickled to hear an actress by the Lyceum Theatre declare 'My, what a cute truck'.

Ernest & May's wedding, 2nd June 1920
Laura Ward, Percy Barrand, Ernest Craddock, May Craddock & Henry Rideout
Front – Joyce Fletcher & Margaret Draper

Ernest in his Ford Model T lorry, 1921

CHAPTER FIVE

Scott Road

Around 1922 Ernest, May and Stanley moved from the Norwood estate to another rented property, 164 Scott Road, in order to be closer to the business. The following years brought the family mixed occasions.

During the last two days of June 1923 Ernest's niece, Betty Unwin, spent her tragically short life at her grandparents' home, 407 Earl Marshal Road, where she died of a cerebral haemorrhage and convulsions.

Then, on 23rd December, Joan Hazel Craddock was born to Ernest and May at 164 Scott Road.

Aged over sixty when he purchased his properties, Joseph Craddock continued in the employ of the Midland Railway Company until, following the strike of 1919, he retired at the age of seventy-two. At 407 Earl Marshal Road Joseph tended his vegetable plot and sat with his wife Kate beside the fire with Jimmy their caged canary overhead.

In April 1924 Joseph visited Fir Vale Hospital on two occasions concerning an intestinal obstruction. On 26th of that month he re-entered the hospital but returned home on 1st May. Joseph's niece, Olive French, recalled that her father, Tom Merrick, persuaded the local publican to open his premises so that he could give his dying brother-in-law a last favourite pint. Ernest was present at 407 Earl Marshal Road when his father died on 6th May. Seventy-six was a good age for the time, particularly when taking into account Joseph's life journey from Kettering Union workhouse to Sheffield engine driver and property owner.

Shortly after the death of her father, Nellie Unwin became critically ill with peritonitis. Her sister, Edith Robinson, moved to 407 Earl Marshal Road to help her mother with her care but it was to no avail. Tragically, Nellie died aged just thirty-four, a year to the day after the death of her only child.

When the tenancy of 168 Scott Road became available, the Craddock family moved next door to Henry and Emily Rideout at no.170. From that time Ernest paid rent to his in-laws next door.

Since the business required regular coal deliveries, Ernest could not afford the time for holidays. He would take his family to the coast and stay a night before returning to Sheffield and collect them a week later. The family stayed at boarding houses in Bridlington and Scarborough and also at Cleethorpes and Theddlethorpe on occasions. Ernest took his golf clubs to Theddlethorpe and also played a little golf at Beauchief and Tinsley in Sheffield but had to give up due to lack of time. However, in about 1930, Ernest played with the Hunsley Street chapel cricket team for a brief period when they were in need of a captain. During the vogue for fretwork, he made a wireless cabinet front using Howard Robinson's handicraft set.

In the summer of 1929 Stanley and Joan went to Bridlington with their aunt and uncle, Edith and Willie Robinson, and their children, Howard and Peggy. Soon after they returned home May introduced them to their baby brother, Peter Ernest Craddock, who was born at 168 Scott Road on 3rd September.

Around 1932 Ernest occasionally accompanied Stanley to Sutherland Road baths for a swim before commencing his day's work. Ernest also enjoyed the open-air pools at Scarborough and Cleethorpes.

Three days before Christmas 1932 Ernest's mother died at the Robinson's home, 268 Ellesmere Road. The Craddock family home, 407 Earl Marshal Road, was then let.

That year Ernest purchased his first car, a 1924 Austin open tourer. Private cars were still quite rare in the district so Ernest would occasionally hire his out to take people on holiday and collect them afterwards. He would also give some of the children of the neighbourhood a lift up the road.

Later that decade, Ernest owned an Austin Heavy Twelve Saloon for which he made conical flower holders from aluminium sheet that could be attached to the windows with rubber suction cups. Thus, with the car decked out with bed sheets and white ribbons it was pressed into service for weddings.

He also occasionally taught others to drive. George Goodman, a decorator, had no aptitude whatsoever but school teacher Miss Ethel Roebuck was made of sterner stuff. Stanley and Joan tried their best to contain their mirth as they were bounced around on the back seat. Stanley was fifteen when his father gave him his first driving lesson on a quiet country road.

Ernest endeavoured to attend the Yorkshire Dragoon's Old Comrades' Association monthly meetings and the annual dinners. Upon his return, usually from the Bay Horse on Pitsmoor Road, he took great care not to wake the rest of the household.

Clarry Gilliat, an old 4th Trooper, was a farmer who lived at Yew Tree Farm at Auckley near Doncaster and later at nearby Mosham Farm. Over the following years, the Craddock family enjoyed visiting their mixed farm and receiving the Gilliats' hospitality. Clarry's wife, Bertha, was a good cook, and their family of Don, Joan and Neal, were of similar ages to the Craddock children. Clarry's party piece was to 'play the cat'. Having caught a farmyard moggie, Clarry held it under his arm and bit the animal's tail whilst regulating the resultant screech in the manner of a bagpipe.

Stanley attended Firth Park Secondary School from 1932 and matriculated at his school certificate exams in the summer of 1937. Against his parent's wishes, he insisted on leaving school the following year having gained references from his headmaster and the Rev. James Wallace of St. James' Church. Stanley joined the sales department of the mining machinery company, Hardy Patent Pick.

Sheffield Wednesday Football Club was the winner of the Football Association cup in 1935. Peter vividly remembered his father taking him to the city centre to see a huge crowd cheer the victorious Owls.

Henry Rideout's health eventually declined to the point when he was confined to his bed on the ground floor front room where he was cared for by his wife and daughter. As 1937 drew to a close, a small Christmas tree was bought for Henry but he died on 1st December aged just sixty-seven.

In the new year it was decided that the Craddock family would move into 170 Scott Road with May's mother to allow 168 to be let again. Since 170 had just two bedrooms, Emily and Joan had to share whilst Stanley and Peter occupied the attic.

170 had two cellars, one into which coal was delivered and a food cellar behind with a stone slab and a safe in which food was preserved. Ernest made the food safe from what had been intended to be a boot for the car with the addition of some perforated zinc sheeting.

Ernest was a capable and practical man but he always employed local tradesmen to decorate and conduct other work on his properties. Also, May wanted him to rest during his time off work. Each Friday night Ernest would return home with a bar of chocolate for everyone bought from a customer's sweet shop. Alcohol was generally only consumed at Christmas and, then, not in much quantity for no more reason than Ernest and May preferred to spend their money on other things.

In the summer of 1938 whilst Stanley holidayed in Skegness with some friends, Joan and Peter accompanied the Robinson family to North Wales and in August May gave birth to a baby girl at Marlcliffe Nursing Home. Perhaps as a consolation for losing his position as the youngest member of the family, Peter was asked to choose the name: Anne Patricia Craddock.

The Craddock family at the seaside in the 1930s

CHAPTER SIX

The Second World War

The approaching conflict with Germany was more evident to the general public than the Great War had been a quarter of a century earlier.

In 1938 Stanley went to the drill hall at Middlewood with the intention of enlisting in the Royal Artillery but he was deemed to be too young to join without his parents' permission. Ernest told him that his mother, who had lost many male acquaintances during the last war, was worried about him.

Despite that, as soon as he turned eighteen in April 1939, Stanley joined his father's old unit, 'A' Squadron, the Queen's Own Yorkshire Dragoons. He participated in their Whitsuntide annual camp at Fourstones Park, Newbrough, near Hexham where recollection of Ernest's earlier service inevitably meant that Stanley would be known as 'Young Craddock'.

In Sheffield the family was provided with gas-masks. They were selected for fit to obtain the correct seal and contained in a cardboard box that had to be carried at all times. Baby Anne was provided with a version that enveloped the upper part of her body; air was supplied by means of a hand-operated pump. Anne made it perfectly clear what she thought of the apparatus. With conflict imminent, May insisted that professional photographs were taken of the group of four siblings.

War with Germany was declared on 3rd September 1939, Peter's tenth birthday. That day the family drove to Darley Dale where Joan and Peter were to stay with Ernest's cousin, Ted Milner, and his family. That night the air-raid sirens sounded for the first time.

Back in Sheffield, Ernest's Bedford lorry was commandeered but it was never explained how halting a family business and depriving hundreds of homes of coal would assist with the war effort. Thankfully Ernest managed to locate his lorry and retrieve it from the Fire Service. Coal was put on ration and customers were obliged to register with a particular merchant. That had the benefit of reducing bad debts since there was no longer the option of transferring to another source of supply.

During the first half of September 'A' Squadron of the Yorkshire Dragoons was based at Norbury Hall, the drill hall, off Barnsley Road. Then the whole regiment moved to various villages near Malton where they received their horses. 'A' Squadron, based at Hovingham in Yorkshire, was visited by the family. A few Great War veterans including Ernest and Captain Matt Sheppard borrowed some of the fine Worcestershire hunters and Ernest had his first ride since the Great War.

Ernest, May and Anne visited Joan and Peter at Darley Dale at weekends when the petrol ration allowed them to make the journey. Then, after a few weeks, Joan returned to Sheffield to take up a job in the photograph and print room at the English Steel Corporation where Ernest's life-long friend, Harry Alvey, was the chief engineer. Peter arrived back at no. 170 in time for Christmas when 'Father Christmas' noisily dropped a no. 5 Meccano set down the attic stairs.

The family acquired a budgerigar which they named Cobber after Cobber Kain the New Zealand fighter pilot ace who was killed in a flying accident in June 1940.

Throughout the war a sign was displayed over the kitchen mantelpiece that read:

May put up black-out curtains and Ernest devised a mechanism that lowered a tin over the kitchen light whenever the outside door was opened. He removed the rockery in the back yard, dug a huge hole and erected an Anderson air-raid shelter with a blast wall in front of the door made by filling a bent steel sheet with soil and rubble. He then fitted out the shelter with a sump, plank floor, benches and a cupboard.

Ernest's nephew, Howard Robinson, who had been president of the Sheffield University Student's Union, had a different view of the war.

In April 1940, when Howard turned twenty-five and was required to register for military service, he decided to declare himself a conscientious objector. Howard stated before a tribunal in Leeds that he objected to military service on Christian grounds and that by joining the armed forces he would be helping to carry on the war. Judge Stewart told him 'Piffle, and you must know it'. After learning of that from the local press, May referred to Howard as Piffle. Ernest generally kept his opinions to himself and was very proud that Stanley was doing his duty.

In June, Howard was called up to serve in the army and, on the basis of his degree and his father's profession as a headmaster, received a commission in the York and Lancaster Regiment in November 1941. Whilst serving in administrative roles, Howard attained the rank of captain.

The Anderson shelter at no. 170 was first put to the test on Anne's second birthday, 18th August 1940, when the air attacks on Sheffield started.

It had been agreed that the Heginbotham couple, the tenants of no. 168, could use the shelter but it was nevertheless a surprise when the family found them installed there when they arrived after dark. They spent that night in darkness, cramped and uncomfortable conditions listening to approaching enemy aircraft and bombs exploding. Ernest gained the impression that the warm weight on his lap was Joan's head until he found that it was a black cat which then made a rapid exit from the shelter. It was perhaps during that long, sleepless night, that Ernest conceived a scheme for improving their shelter arrangements.

Ernest bricked up their cellar ground-level window, reinforced the ceiling with corrugated iron sheets which were supported by props and installed bunk beds. He then knocked a hole through to the cellar of no. 168 so that if one of the houses was badly damaged it could be used as an alternative escape route. The new tenants, Mr. & Mrs. Brown, shared the shelter with the Craddock family and when the danger from enemy aircraft diminished one of the adults would go upstairs to brew a pot of tea.

Ernest didn't join the Local Defence Volunteers (later renamed the Home Guard) due to what he perceived as the snobbery of rank based on position in civilian life. However, he was a street warden and was on hand when needed. He was issued with a composition helmet, acquired a stirrup pump and SP was painted on the house wall to indicate the fact. From the ARP wardens' post on Ellesmere Road, Ernest learned the degree of air-raid alert from lamps placed outside the wardens' post rising from all-clear, to amber, purple and red.

When Ernest and Joan visited the Storer's house on Scott Road to use their billiards table the air-raid siren sounded and they had to hastily return home. Ernest also honed his skills with a cue at the billiards table that was housed in the large attic of Harry and Nora Alvey's home in Ringinglow Road. Peter recalled the occasion when his father let him have a go by pointing where to hit the ball 'with his work-gnarled finger'.

In 1943 Ernest was promoted from section leader to street captain for Scott Road up to the cemetery gates. He joked in a letter to Stanley that he thought that the uniform was a white jacket with three pips and crossed stirrup pumps on each shoulder!

Stanley, being too young to serve overseas with the Yorkshire Dragoons, was transferred to a light AA regiment of the Royal Artillery and posted to an installation on the outskirts of Sheffield. Later in the war he served with the First Army in North Africa, the Fifth Army in Italy and the 13th Infantry Division in Greece.

After owning a succession of Austin Heavy Twelves, in 1940 Ernest bought a smaller car to economise on petrol, a 1938 Austin 10.

In 1941 the petrol ration for private cars was stopped but continued for motorcycles for another six months. For that reason Ernest bought a Matchless 500 motorcycle in the summer. On one memorable occasion he hurtled along the yard and across the street as he grappled with the clutch. Having mastered the machine, Peter rode pillion with him into Derbyshire but after conking out, the motorcycle returned to Sheffield on the back of a GPO lorry. Despite that setback Stanley found the bike useful when he returned home on leave.

During the Sheffield Blitz of 12th/13th December 1940, Ernest remained at no. 170 whilst his family stayed with the Ward family at Birley Carr in the rural outskirts of Sheffield. (Fred Ward was the father of May's friend and matron of honour at her wedding.) Stanley arrived home on leave to find all the windows broken and soot blown down the chimney making the house temporarily uninhabitable.

The family moved to a farm near to the Wards' house that was run by Mrs. Sellars and her sons, Thompson and John. Ernest equipped himself with several mouse traps with which he hoped to control the vermin that were prevalent in the old farm house. The family eventually returned to no. 170 but May's mother, Emily Rideout, took a bed-sitting room in Bridge End Farm at

Derwent, a remote village in Derbyshire. (Later in the war she moved to Froggatt Edge.)

On 11th October 1941 Stanley was again at home on leave when there was another air-raid. Ernest was in the road on street duty when he suddenly threw himself onto the ground as a bomb exploded close by. Having shielded his younger sister from the blast, Stanley rushed outside to find his father picking himself up. Their neighbour, Mr. Brown, later told Stanley that he kept an eye on his father knowing that he had some experience of that sort of thing from his service in the Great War. Ernest and Stanley started to lift away the remains of a nearby house in which they suspected that someone was still alive. To their annoyance, when the emergency services arrived, they were asked to move away. Kenneth Middleton, who had been sheltering under their kitchen sink, was the only survivor of his family of four. Four members of the Tempest family next door were killed leaving a young boy survivor. After that air raid the house was again temporarily uninhabitable and Peter was put up by the Woodcock family in Bents Drive, close to his school. May's cousin, Douglas Woodcock, ran his family's travel company which had been founded by his father, G.A. Woodcock.

Coal was scarce during the winter of 1942/3. However, whenever Ernest had secured some coal he was loath to turn down other work because he might not be offered it again when he had no coal.

In March 1943, lacking a mate, Peter held bags open as his father filled them and the following month the pair took a load of coke to the Toledo steel works. In a letter to Stanley, Peter described the crucible steel-making process they were shown by the foreman.

Having passed his half-century, May tried to persuade Ernest to sell the business so that they could retire to somewhere pleasant such as the Hope Valley. However, Ernest's initial enquiries revealed that his business might only realise £100. However, an advertisement that summer generated eleven enquiries including several from the city's large coal merchants. One coal dealer suggested merging his one hundred and fifty customer concern with Ernest's four hundred customer business but nothing came of it. Ernest claimed, in a letter to Stanley, that if he had the chance of a decent permanent job he would sell up. A major problem was securing reliable labour. Peter helped out occasionally with light duties when Ernest was without his mate Bob, until a new man, freshly discharged from the army, took his place in August.

One day that summer Ernest's brother-in-law, Willie Robinson entertained the Craddock family at their home *Redcote,* 14 Crabtree Lane. Willie, an elementary school headmaster, enjoyed organising games of skittles on the veranda, and also darts, clock golf and croquet in their large garden.

In August Ernest again found himself without coal, but a firm wanted a lorry to take two and three quarter tons of steel bars to Ecclesfield. He was a little concerned about the length of the bars but the weight should have been within the capacity of his Bedford lorry. However, he had driven no more than four hundred yards when he heard a great cracking sound and so brought his lorry to an abrupt halt. Upon investigation he discovered that the two main chassis beams had broken leaving the lorry badly bent. Ernest reversed back into the yard and the load was removed. The site manager found two flat steel bars from a warehouse that were cut to length and suggested that Ernest enquire at a firm in the next street about drilling them so that they could be bolted to the chassis. The firm was short of labour but Ernest was allowed to use their facilities to drill the holes himself and he returned the next morning to complete the job. Pleased with the result, Ernest claimed in a letter to Stanley that the lorry was stronger than ever! It was what Ernest would have called 'All Sir Garnet', a byword for success referring to the efficient and successful Victorian general, Sir Garnet Wolseley. Presumably, Ernest was then able to deliver the bars without further mishap.

Due to the wartime scarcities, in September father and son converted an old radio crystal set box into a sewing box to present to Anne at Christmas. Ernest sawed, sanded and stained and Peter decorated the lid with a fairy on a toadstool. Nearly eighty years later Anne continues to use the same box.

In October Ernest and Peter queued at the Town Hall for thirty-five minutes to be rewarded with a thirty-five second sight of the Stalingrad Sword, the British crafted treasure that was to be presented to the people of that city. With nearly two hundred people passing by each minute, Ernest was disappointed not to have had a proper look at the elaborate engraving. May wasn't bothered and reported in a letter to Stanley that Anne wouldn't go if she wasn't able to touch it!

Ernest had become acquainted with Charlie Bufton, the manager of Morton & Storer, through occasional work transporting Derbyshire limestone. They had similar values and became good friends. Through his work, Charlie knew the local Imperial Chemical Industries (ICI) representative and was impressed with his station in life. Having learned that a new ICI office was to be opened in Sheffield in the new year, he persuaded Ernest that could be an ideal opportunity for Peter.

Ernest and May spent some restless nights discussing the issue. May was against the idea but, swayed by her husband, was comforted by her thinking that 'all happens for the best'. Stanley, away on active service, wrote to his parents to try to dissuade them from taking his brother out of his grammar school but it was to no avail. Ernest wrote to Peter's headmaster stating that his absence on the day of his interview was unavoidable. Ernest paid the ten pound fine to take him out of school and Peter joined ICI at 285 Glossop Road at the age of fourteen and a half.

Peter's interest in chemistry was initiated by his chemistry teacher and given fresh impetus by his job with ICI. As he conducted experiments at a washstand in the attic of no. 170, occasional explosions emanated from the back yard. Ernest and May were very tolerant of Peter's activities that they probably thought were related to his work. Later Ernest helped Peter fit out the loft over the garage (originally the stable) into a proposed plastics factory.

Ernest had great difficulty finding, and then keeping, workmates during the war.

There was George, a large but simple man, who complained to May that Anne, when a toddler, had pinched his lunch sandwiches. In a letter, Ernest told Stanley that he couldn't make up his mind whether to try to expand the business or to sell up. He was finding the work hard but the remuneration was good so he wondered about specialising in haulage. He had heard that men up to the age of fifty-five were being recruited into certain branches of the RAF and he quite fancied the idea of a comfortable job back in the forces.

In March 1944 workmate Ernest Buxton applied to Firth Brown's steel works but having learned that they had no job for him he returned to 170 Scott Road. Buxton was an excitable fellow and Ernest really wanted someone who would be more loyal.

As the war drew to a close, Ernest acquired an Austin five-ton lorry for which he extended the garage. Ever the practical man, Ernest renovated Peter's bicycle for Anne and made her a dolls push-chair out of riveted mild steel strip.

On VE Day the blackouts were replaced with flags and bunting and Ernest and Peter drove into town where the former had to discourage a few over-excited youths from standing on his car bumper. Then, in June Ernest found the time to accompany the family to Blackpool.

CHAPTER SEVEN

Abbeyfield Road

Stanley returned home to 170 Scott Road on 12th May 1946 fit, tanned and six foot three. As he and Peter shared the attic again they caught up with their very different experiences of the war.

In June the whole family went to Bournemouth, their only holiday when all were present from start to end. Due to the demands of the business it was also Ernest's first holiday for twenty-four years.

The winter of 1946/7 was exceptionally severe and Polish troops were deployed to try to keep Sheffield's roads and rail lines open. Despite the shortage of coal, Ernest's services were in great demand. He hung a fire from the lorry's tail board to try to keep both coal bags and hands usable. Ernest did not want either of his sons to join the business due to the unrelenting, hard, physical work; he wanted Stanley and Peter to pursue professions.

Ernest's workmate failed to turn up on 20th November 1947, Princess Elizabeth's wedding day, when Stanley helped his father out. Ernest was reluctant at first but Stanley enjoyed the novelty. On another occasion when Ernest was ill he refused Peter's offer of help. Ernest had been known to work through a bout of flu, an activity that very likely caused permanent damage to his heart.

With the newfound freedom of the post war years, Peter accompanied his father to a football international at Hampden Park in Glasgow. Later, in the early 1950s, the pair saw the new Queen and Winston Churchill at Doncaster racecourse on a rare and special outing on St. Legers' Day.

Stanley found it difficult to settle back into his civilian job at Hardy Patent Pick; he told Peter that had done quite enough digging in the army! So, when he learned that a friend was proposing to train to be a school teacher he decided to join him. After a period of training, Stanley started at Woodseats School to the south-west of the city on 1st March 1948. To the slight annoyance of his uncle Willie Robinson, who had been a long-standing and active member of the National Union of Teachers, Stanley joined the National Association of Schoolmasters and always insisted that he was a schoolmaster.

Peter took heed of Stanley's advice not to join the army and hoped that the RAF might provide a more varied and comfortable existence for his two years of National Service. In the autumn of 1947 a photographic portrait of Peter wearing his RAF beret arrived at home and was duly framed and displayed on the dining room wall. After training to be a wireless operator, Peter was based at Boston in Lincolnshire with an air/sea rescue unit onboard a launch that patrolled The Wash for downed aircrew.

In January 1948 May placed an advertisement in the *Sheffield Telegraph* to try to find the family a new home.

At an auction in February, Ernest was prepared to pay £2,000 for a house but instead came away with a watch! Two or three properties were viewed including 206 Barnsley Road which had a cellar kitchen that May likened to a dungeon. She then decided to place another advertisement, that time in *The Star*.

The house-hunting was initiated by Joan's relationship with Philip Wade who, in May, asked Ernest for his daughter's hand. Three months later, when Ernest drove to Doncaster to do some work for Charlie Bufton, his friend gave him a case of cutlery for the couple. The Buftons residence at 32 Abbeyfield Road may have initiated their interest in the properties of that nearby road.

Joan and Philip's wedding, on 4th September, was conducted at St. James' Church in Scott Road. Peter, acting as an usher in his RAF uniform, handed out hymn sheets whilst Anne was a bridesmaid. As well as the usual photographs, one was taken of Ernest flanked by his tall sons. Ernest, who was measured as five feet seven and a half inches during the Great War, joked that he felt that he had been arrested.

The reception was held at St. Cuthbert's Church hall where Ernest, daunted by the prospect of making a speech as the father of the bride, persuaded Willie Robinson to speak in his stead. After the nuptials the couple moved into rented rooms at 745 Ecclesfield Road whilst Ernest, May and Anne holidayed in Bournemouth.

In a letter to Peter in October, Ernest mentioned that he got on well with his workmate Albert and joked that the blot on the envelope must have been done in the post.

Ernest's sister, Edith Robinson, died on 15th December when ten-year-old Anne witnessed her father's tears of sorrow.

In February 1949 Ernest claimed that he had two good lads working for him, presumably Albert and Fred. He got on well with both but Ernest was concerned that Fred would go back to working for his father who was also a coal dealer. Ernest accompanied them on the rounds but didn't carry bags since that activity was wearing him out.

Removal from Scott Road took place in August when Ernest coordinated the extraction of a bulky wardrobe from the attic. Peter lowered the piece of furniture by rope out of the window to Stanley who was standing on a very ancient and distinctly short ladder that was supported by the bed of the lorry.

Joan and Philip moved into 170 Scott Road as the rest of the family took up residence in the newly purchased semi-detached villa with a garage, 278 Abbeyfield Road. That house, Ernest's first property purchase, included a plot of land on the corner with Osgathorpe Road where two houses were later built. Ernest garaged his car to the rear of their new house but continued to keep the lorry at 170 Scott Road.

When Cobber, the blue budgie, died he was replaced a week later by New Cobber, a Green Un' (after the Sheffield sporting newspaper) after the family had been informed that green budgerigars were hardier. Shortly after, as Ernest, May and Anne returned from a trip to Chatsworth they stopped to help two cyclists who had been hurt in a crash. Leaving Anne and Jill, their newly acquired pedigree Scottie, with their machines, Ernest and May conveyed the injured cyclists to a surgery. As May escorted them into the building, Ernest drove back to collect Anne and Jill.

During the move to Abbeyfield Road, May dealt with a singular duty.

She had long been acquainted with Miss Elizabeth Russell, a lady of about May's mother's age, who had cleaned for various members of her family in the past. May occasionally helped to carry Miss Russell's shopping back to her tiny and scruffy house at 5 Stockton Street. Depending on the availability of petrol, Ernest or Stanley would sometimes drive May over. The house had no electricity and Miss Russell considered the illumination provided by a street lamp to be quite adequate.

After Miss Russell suffered a fall, May visited her in hospital and, to alleviate the older lady's concern, May agreed to fetch 'the money' from 5 Stockton Street. However, when she handing it over, Miss Russell became agitated and insisted that there was more than the twenty pounds or so that May had brought. Indeed there was and a further search resulted in hundreds of gold sovereigns and half-sovereigns bursting from rotten bags onto the dining room table at 170 Scott Road.

When Miss Russell died in July 1949, May, as the sole executor of her will, was tasked with taking it to probate and, to that end, communicated with members of Miss Russell's family until the end of the year. All agreed that their relative had been foolish to live in squalor as she did whilst in possession of such wealth. However, Miss Russell had insisted it was 'family money' that could not be touched in her lifetime.

Acting on advice from her bank, May went to the Sheffield Smelting Company where someone she knew helped her deal with the near two thousand pounds worth of coins.

On 12th August 1950 Peter acted as Stanley's best man at his wedding to Eileen Hall at St. Cuthbert's Church.

At the end of October, Ernest and Stanley marched with fellow ex-servicemen past the saluting base at the Mansion House in Doncaster. They made their way to St. George's Church for the unveiling of a memorial to the Yorkshire Dragoons who had been lost during the war. Captain Matt Sheppard was present at the Brightside Conservative & Liberal Association annual ball in the Cutlers' Hall in November to which Stanley and Eileen were also invited. The couple lodged with fellow school teacher, Miss Edith Roebuck, at 164 Scott Road for about a year before moving into a semi-detached house, 43 Hemper Lane in Bradway which was conveniently situated for Stanley's daily drive to Woodseats School.

After Peter completed his National Service in the RAF he moved into the new family home in Abbeyfield Road whilst he worked at the ICI offices in Sheffield. Reorganisation resulted in his transfer to Manchester so he spent just the weekends at home whilst he commuted across the Pennines.

That June, as the Korean War raged in the Far East, Peter was recalled from the RAF reserve for a fortnight's training at RAF Box near Chippenham in Wiltshire to replace men who had been sent out to the conflict. After returning to Sheffield, Peter accompanied his parents, Anne, Stanley and Eileen to Dover for a week.

Ernest and May's first grandchild, Elizabeth Wade, was born in March 1952. Ernest told Stanley, 'Look at that. Only just here but one of us already'.

May's mother, Emily Rideout, took to her bed as an elderly invalid where she occupied the front ground floor room at 278 Abbeyfield Road. She was provided with a bell with which she could summon assistance. In the middle of one night Emily rang the bell and told May that someone had been in her room. May was shocked at the possibility but then discovered that either she or Ernest had forgotten to lock the kitchen door. May locked it, bolted the scullery door and returned to bed without ever telling Ernest.

In common with many households, a television set was acquired to watch the Queen's Coronation in June 1953. Ernest enjoyed televised football matches and shuffled his feet with the flow of the game.

Susan Wade was born on 3rd September 1954 at 170 Scott Road. She was, to the day, a quarter of a century her Uncle Peter's junior who was appointed her godfather.

A diagnosis of angina that year may have persuaded Ernest to write his will. However, his condition did not discourage him from buying a new model Austin A50 the following year.

In February 1955 the Wade family left 170 Scott Road for 22 Conalan Avenue in Bradway, less than a mile from Stanley and Eileen's home in Hemper Lane.

In April, Bert Unwin and his second wife Winnie were visiting 278 Abbeyfield Road when Peter introduced them to Kay Hulse. A few days later

Ernest, May and Anne visited Kay's home, an imposing semi-detached Victorian villa, opposite Dore & Totley railway station. Although Ernest enjoyed a drink or two at regimental reunions, alcohol was rarely consumed at home so Anne's first taste of an alcoholic drink, offered by Kay's father, became a lasting memory.

In the month of May all the family were at 278 Abbeyfield Road to meet Kay at May's birthday tea. Then, whilst Peter did most of the driving, parents and siblings toured the Lake District for three days at the end of the month prior to Peter's second transfer from Sheffield to the ICI office in Manchester.

May's mother, Emily Rideout, was dangerously ill in hospital by mid June and she died on 21st aged eighty-three.

In July Ernest, May and Anne embarked on a coach tour to Paris, Brussels and Le Touquet. Ignoring appeals to refrain, Ernest couldn't resist trying out a few of the French phrases he had picked up during the Great War forty years before. However, as he told them, his linguistic knowledge got them around Paris.

In the autumn Peter became engaged to Kay Hulse who insisted that he gave up smoking. When Ernest learned that, he decided to do likewise and persuaded Stanley to give up as well. Thereafter Ernest generally only smoked on special occasions.

May's birthday coincided with Whit Monday in 1956 when the family, including Peter and Kay, visited Ted and Edie Milner in Darley Dale. Ernest enjoyed visiting the Whitworth Institute in Darley Dale to play billiards and snooker with Ted. The cousins also attended cricket matches at Bramall Lane and in Chesterfield.

Hazel Wade was born on 4th June 1956, twelve days before Peter and Kay's wedding at St. John's Church in Abbeydale. Stanley was the best man and Anne a bridesmaid. After the nuptials the couple lodged in Burnage as they both worked in Manchester. Later that year Peter and Kay moved into a newly built semi-detached house in Etchells Road, Heald Green, to the south of Manchester and Ernest, May and Anne regularly drove over to visit.

In September it was discovered that their Scottie, Jill, was so 'full of tumours' that the vet didn't allow her to come out of the anaesthetic. The following month her place in the household was taken by May's choice of a Scottie bitch puppy called Judy.

Ernest sold the coal merchant business when he reached the state pension age in July 1957.

The final weekend was very busy as Ernest and May had three-year-old Susan Wade staying with them and people called in to settle their bills. May, who occasionally left her rings lying around in the kitchen, then discovered that they were missing. The police were called and a detective asked May if she could suggest a likely suspect from their list of customers. May refused to speculate, concerned that she could blight someone's life. Ernest told her that the rings were only baubles and May accepted the loss. What May could not understand was that she thought that Judy was a good house dog and wondered whether she had known the thief.

In July 1958 Ernest and May stayed in a flat in Scarborough that May judged to be not her favourite seaside resort. The primary purpose was to visit Bert and Winnie Unwin at their retirement home. With forty-one stairs up to their flat, Ernest tried to limit the climb to once a day.

The following month they placed an advertisement in the *Sheffield Telegraph* with the objective of selling their house. As Ernest's heart condition worsened both were keen to move to a bungalow.

Joan & Philip Wade's wedding
4th September 1948

Joan & Ernest

Stanley, Ernest & Peter
May, Anne & Emily Rideout

CHAPTER EIGHT

Hemper Lane

Ernest, May and Anne moved into what was to become known to the family as 'the bungalow', 14 Hemper Lane, in Bradway in late August 1958.

Purchased from a Miss Lake for £2,600, their new home had been built in 1924 and was situated directly across the road from Stanley and Eileen's house at no. 43. A narrow drive led to the garage at no.14 that adjoined the left-hand side of the bungalow which was fronted by crazy paving and a low wall. The front garden contained several mature apple trees screened from the road by a row of tall poplar trees.

The back garden could be accessed around the right-hand side of the bungalow and also through the garage. A privet hedge divided the formal back garden from the lower kitchen garden which contained a cluster of apple trees and a greenhouse and was bounded by another row of poplar trees. A small building to the rear of the garage became Ernest's workshop. Next to that, screened from the formal garden by a trellis, were assorted sheds that contained garden equipment such as a garden tent and Ernest's wartime stirrup pump.

From the front door of the bungalow, a tee-shaped hallway led to three bedrooms, bathroom, dining room and a sitting room at the back. The last was lined with oak panels and bayed French windows gave access to the back garden down a short flight of steps. A small and poorly laid-out kitchen could be entered from the sitting and dining rooms with an external door next to the garage door.

Stanley and Eileen's adopted son, James, and his cousin John, Peter and Kay's first child, were christened together at St. James' Church on 28th September.

In November the family had problems with the lights in the bungalow. Anne and Stanley replaced bulbs and fuses then Ernest's discovery of poor wiring made them wonder if re-wiring would be necessary. To add to his concerns, Ernest cut his eye-lid whilst chopping wood (May had told him not to) and then he dropped a hammer on his toe in the garage.

Those misfortunes however, did not prevent Ernest and May from going to the Manchester College of Science and Technology at the beginning of December to witness Peter being presented as an Associate of the College.

Towards the end of the year Anne surprised her parents by announcing her engagement to Bryan Hodgson. May hoped that they would be sensible and wait a year or so before getting married.

With Stanley and his family just across the road and Joan and her family less than a mile away, family gatherings at the bungalow could be organised relatively easily. Peter and his family travelled from Heald Green by train until, with Philip Wade's guidance, they acquired a Ford Popular at Easter 1959.

Boxing Day parties at the bungalow became established with Ernest presiding over much of the fun and games. A family favourite was 'ring on a string'; Ernest threaded his signet ring onto a long loop of string that was held by participants in both hands as they sat around the sitting room. One of those hands concealed the ring from a grandchild who task it was to glance around from inside the loop as they decided whose hand to lightly tap. Once tapped, the owner was obliged to open it to reveal whether or not they were concealing the ring. Once the ring had been found other grandchildren were only too eager to have a go.

Ernest enjoyed mystifying his family with his 'magic writing' as he tapped a poker on the hearth a number of times to indicate a word. Also, the family were asked to 'guess' the number of coins that had been concealed beneath the hearth rug. Upon leaving the room Ernest pulled the door closed using a number of fingers that indicated how many coins were to be placed under the rug by someone who was in on the trick.

Ever since the cricket and football days of his youth, Ernest enjoyed practicing his hand-and-eye coordination skills. He would try to light-heartedly alarm May by dropping an egg over his shoulder and then catch it with his other hand. The occasion when the egg broke when it landed on his signet ring caused general hilarity. A quoits board was hung on the kitchen door onto which Ernest threw rubber rings. Stanley's old riding crop also hung from the door with which Ernest tried to deter local boys from venturing into the front garden to steal apples from his trees.

On 18th April 1959 Ernest and Clarry Gilliat attended the Yorkshire Dragoons' Regimental Association annual dinner in Doncaster. The Earl of Scarbrough, the mayor of Doncaster and Captain Matt Sheppard appeared with other Great War veterans in a photograph which was published in the *Doncaster Chronicle*. The next day Ernest and Stanley joined the parade when the guidon (the colours of a dragoon regiment) was laid up in St. George's Church. With the reduction of the strength of the Territorial Army, the regiment was absorbed into the Queen's Own Yorkshire Yeomanry.

At the end of the month of May, Ernest and May embarked on a coach tour through France to spend a week in Interlaken in Switzerland. From there they were conveyed to the Blue Lake, ventured on Lake Lucerne in a pedalo and were carried up a mountain in a chair-lift. Whilst they were away, Dinky, their budgie was cared for by Miss Heginbotham.

Peter's job with ICI required him to attend a course on plastics in Welwyn Garden City for most of August. Kay and John stayed at the bungalow for the duration to where Peter returned each weekend. It was during that stay that Kay told the family that she was expecting another child.

Anne's twenty-first birthday was celebrated by a lunch at the *Maynard Arms* in Grindleford. Stanley presided over the event where Ernest gained the impression that all the young men present were over six feet in height.

In November the family was lucky to escape injury when a light fitting fell onto the kitchen table and smashed several pots. That same month Ernest had more repairs to do when he replaced some greenhouse panes. (A gale later caused a complete collapse of the structure.)

When complications developed during Kay's second pregnancy she spent extended periods at Stepping Hill Hospital in Stockport. As Peter worked in Manchester, John was cared for at the bungalow and by his maternal grandparents at *Woodlands* in Dore. Luckily, the houses were situated only about a mile apart via the steep and winding Twentywell Lane.

John occupied the front bedroom in the bungalow from where he would toddle into his Auntie Anne's bedroom. Each morning he would wave to Anne as she set out for work and also to his Uncle Stanley as he drove off to his school. Ernest's activities, particularly those in his workshop, fascinated the little lad. May wrote that Ernest missed John when he was not there but at least he could then rely on his tools being where he had left them. Occasionally John was taken to spend the day at 22 Conalan Avenue with his Auntie Joan and cousins, Elizabeth, Susan and Hazel.

Having done Littlewood's pools for many years, Ernest was interested to learn that their neighbour-to-be had won £102,000 by that means just before Christmas 1959. Their outgoing neighbours were understandably annoyed that they had agreed to reduce the asking price for their bungalow by fifty pounds. In the new year of 1960 Judy caused their new neighbours' Siamese cat to climb a poplar tree obliging the owner to get out his ladder. May noted that John was getting more used to Judy though the dog tended to get rather too close to him for his liking.

In March, Louise, Stanley and Eileen's adopted daughter, was christened and later that month Ernest and May drove to Stockport to visit Kay in hospital. A few days later they set out for another hospital, in Swallownest, to visit Polly Hazell, May's mother's cousin. Being unfamiliar with the district, Ernest drove the wrong way along a one-way street where they had the misfortune to encounter a police car. Sadly, Polly, an elderly long-term mental patient, did not appreciate their visit.

On Stanley's thirty-ninth birthday, 12th April, Peter and Kay arrived at the bungalow to introduce John to his brother Philip and then the family drove home to Heald Green.

In June 1960 Ernest and May celebrated their ruby wedding anniversary in the company of their family and with Willie and Peggy Robinson and Bryan Hodgson. Photographs of the group were taken by Philip Wade and Peggy Robinson and then of Ernest and May with their seven grandchildren.

During the second half of July Ernest and May embarked on a driving tour around Scotland. They saw a little of the Highland Games, visited Oban, Glencoe and Fort William and viewed Ben Nevis from afar. They also went to Fort Augustus, Loch Ness, Inverness and Peebles and returned via Barnard Castle and Harrogate.

On 3rd September Anne and Bryan married at St. James's Church with the reception held at St. Andrew's Hotel in Kenwood Road. The couple set up home in Wollaton Road near Totley Rise and their twin sons, Richard and Andrew, were born in December 1961.

May noted in December 1960 that Ernest was finding that even a little gardening was too much for him. They employed contractors to remove two large poplar trees on the right hand side of the bungalow.

May's aunt by marriage, Doris Rideout (Frank's widow), lived in High Trees in Dore village. In January 1961 Doris tried to interest May and Ernest in building a pair of flats in Drury Lane. She suggested that they could occupy the ground floor flat whilst Doris and her sister shared the upper flat. However, Ernest was not keen on the area and May was sceptical that the land was available.

In June, Stanley was driving his father in his car when they noticed smoke coming out from under the bonnet. After coming to a halt outside West Bar police station they discovered electrical insulation ablaze that necessitated a tow to a garage and an expensive wiring loom to be replaced.

On 23rd July Ernest, Stanley and Eileen viewed 66 Furniss Avenue in Dore as a prospective new home for Peter, Kay and their sons who intended to move back to Sheffield. From the end of September into October, the family had a three week stay at the bungalow whilst Ernest and May were away in Eastbourne and work was done on their new house in Furniss Avenue.

Shortly after Ernest and May returned to the bungalow George Fletcher stayed with them for a few days. When they lived in Scott Road and Abbeyfield Road, George, who was May's uncle by marriage, would occasionally turn up unannounced from Kempston near Bedford to stay for a few days equipped only with a cut-throat razor and a spare shirt collar.

Ernest and May regularly visited Furniss Avenue where they played Scrabble and cards with Peter and Kay. After a spate of burglaries in Bradway, Ernest and May arrived clutching their metal deeds box.

Yuri Gagarin orbited the earth on Stanley's fortieth birthday, 12th April 1961. Then, on 20th February 1962, Ernest and May listened attentively to the radio coverage of John Glenn's orbital spaceflight.

May enjoyed being by and on the sea and the sight and sound of breaking waves. To that end, in June 1962 she and Ernest boarded the Wilson Line freighter S.S. *Borodino* at Hull bound for Copenhagen. The accommodation was basic but they enjoyed the company of the crew at mealtimes and being rocked to sleep by the motion of the sea. Peter managed to combine a business trip to Hull to collect his parents from the docks and convey them back to Sheffield. They enjoyed the trip so much they repeated it in July 1963.

Ted Milner lost his wife Edie in 1958 and in July 1962 he visited his cousin Ernest and May at the bungalow.

On 27th November 1963, five days after President Kennedy was assassinated, Ernest suffered a heart attack. He was cared for at Wharncliffe hospital in Bradfield until he was discharged on 21st December, James' sixth birthday.

On 11th July 1964 Ernest, May and other members of the family attended Willie Robinson's eightieth birthday party at *Redcote*, 14 Crabtree Lane. Howard and Margaret Robinson and their children, David and Christine, visited from Folkestone and the event was made memorable by the spectacle of eighty candles ablaze on a cake board.

Two days after Ernest celebrated his seventy-second birthday he suffered a partial collapse. However, in August a doctor from Wharncliffe Hospital issued him with a note stating that his high blood pressure was under control and, consequently, was deemed to be fit enough to drive his car.

In July 1965 Ernest and May taught Peter and Kay to play the game of rummy for which the latter bought a baize-faced card table. In September, May persuaded Ernest to spend the morning in bed.

At around that time, Ernest gave John a Ladybird book of railway locomotives and joked with him that since he was born on 17th July, the day before John's birthday, that he was only a day older than his grandson. Later Ernest gave John the German pickelhaube helmet badge he had brought back from the Great War. May later told John that Ernest was particularly keen that he should have it.

At the end of May 1966 Ernest suffered a second heart attack during the morning service at St. James' Church. A friend drove them home in Ernest's car and, despite his condition, Ernest's main concern was that his friend could handle his vehicle. Unfortunately, that was the prelude to a long stay in Wharncliffe hospital during the run-up to his seventy-fourth birthday.

Anne, Bryan and their twin sons moved into a bungalow in Barnsley in December 1963. Their daughter, Caroline, who was born in May 1966, became Ernest and May's tenth and youngest grandchild. Anne was naturally anxious to leave the maternity hospital to visit her father in Wharncliffe where the minister at St. James' Church visited him each day.

In D Ward at Wharncliffe Ernest got to know a fellow patient, William Wardale, who as a keen amateur historian, was intrigued by Ernest's surname and noble brow. After Ernest was discharged on 20th July, Wardale wrote to him concerning his research into Craddock family history. Peter took his parents to visit Wardale and his wife in November and Stanley continued a correspondence that resulted in them receiving a booklet of gleanings concerning the Craddock surname and a skilfully executed depiction of a Craddock coat of arms. Of course, the latter had nothing to do with Ernest's family.

Towards the end of the summer Ernest suffered a minor stroke that left him with slightly impaired vision in his left eye so in October he made the wise decision to sell his car.

In November Ernest received a letter from Captain Matt Sheppard who expressed his disappointment that Ernest was unable to attend the Yorkshire Dragoons annual reunion. However, Captain Matt was pleased to note that Stanley was present.

In 1967 when Ernest learned that Peter, Kay, and their sons were to leave Dore for Malvern, he expressed his concerns to his younger son about the distance from Sheffield. Sadly, Ernest was never able to visit his family in that picturesque part of the country.

Ernest continued to collect the rent from 170 Scott Road until it was sold that year. His parents' old house, 407 Earl Marshal Road, was let until 1976 when Stanley sold the property to a former pupil.

In the spring of 1968 Ernest supervised the lopping of a poplar tree in the front garden. As he and ten-year-old James warned of oncoming traffic, Stanley frantically sawed away at a limb that dropped onto the road.

Judy became quite ancient in dog terms and was taken to the surgery at Batley with a dislocated and partially fractured leg. There she passed away in August aged fourteen.

Later that month, Ernest was admitted to the Royal Hospital in Sheffield suffering from swollen ankles and having coughed up blood. Being unable to pass water, due to an enlarged prostate gland, Ernest faced the dilemma of undergoing surgery or being permanently reliant on a catheter. At a bedside conference with May, Stanley and Peter it was decided that surgery, taking into account Ernest's heart condition, would be too risky. So, newly equipped with a catheter, Ernest and May were able to attend Harry and Nora Alvey's golden wedding celebration at the Rosslyn Court Hotel in Psalter Lane in September. There Ernest was pleased to meet Harry's sister who he had not seen for many years.

In October Ernest enjoyed following the Olympic Games from Mexico City on television. He and May also enjoyed a week in Barnsley with the Hodgson family though one day Ernest had to be taken to a hospital.

At around that time Ernest thanked May for helping with the business; an utterance that had her slightly puzzled.

The catheter caused Ernest much discomfort. On the morning of Christmas Eve Peter took his father to the Royal Hospital concerning a newly fitted appliance and then returned home. That evening, after a glass of brandy had failed to ease the pain, their doctor called for an ambulance and Ernest was conveyed to Wharncliffe Hospital. It was there that Ernest died on 3rd January 1969 of an infection and coronary artery disease at the age of seventy-six.

1959

1960, with grandchildren
James, Susan, Philip, Hazel,
John, Louise & Elizabeth

EPILOGUE

After Ernest passed away, May stayed with Anne and her family in Barnsley and then with Peter and his family in Malvern and, in August 1969, accompanied the latter to Lyme Regis for a week.

Ernest and May had pledged to continue the family parties each Boxing Day as long as one of them remained in the bungalow. Sadly, the following years were marked by May's gradual reduction in mobility due to arthritis that made movement around the bungalow a very slow process. Stanley and his family, just across the road, and Joan and her family, less than a mile away, provided much assistance.

Just when it was hoped that Louise Craddock was on the brink of a promising career as a horsewoman, cancer was diagnosed from which she died in February 1977 aged just seventeen. During that difficult time Stanley relied on May for much moral support.

May became a great-grandmother in June 1977 with the birth of Elizabeth's son, Ben Hukin. Stanley retired as a deputy headmaster in 1981 and May died in 1982 aged eighty-five.

Stanley and Eileen divorced in 1985 and the following year Stanley moved into a bungalow in Huntley Road where he died in 2016 aged ninety-four. Eileen, now ninety-five, continues to live in Sheffield.

After Philip Wade died in 1994 Joan continued to live at 22 Conalan Avenue with the support of her three daughters. Infirmity finally compelled a move to a care home where she died in 2017 aged ninety-three.

Peter's career in the aluminium industry took him and his family to Swansea in 1971 and then to Barton-under-Needwood in Staffordshire in 1981.

Peter retired in 1994 and Kay died in 2001. Peter married Cindy Kettle in 2006 and Peter, now ninety-three, and Cindy continue to live in the same village.

Bryan Hodgson's career with the Midland Bank took him and his family to Newcastle-under-Lyme in 1972 and then to Wilmslow in 1982. In 2020 Anne and Bryan were delighted to receive a card from the Queen to mark their diamond wedding anniversary. Anne is a sprightly eighty-four.

BIBLIOGRAPHY

Craddock, John Peter, He Soldiered under Kitchener,
          The Life and Times of Private Harry Milner of Darley Dale
          Privately produced, 1992

Craddock, J.P., Caradoc's Kin, The Craddock Family of Cranford, Kettering
      & Sheffield, Privately produced,1995 & 2006 and Cade Books, 2020

Craddock, J.P., Sheffield Hero, The Life of Capt. Matt Sheppard
          Pickard Communication, 2007

Craddock, J.P., William Henry Robinson,
      Sheffield Schoolmaster & Educationist, Cade Books, 2018

Craddock, Stanley Rideout, Ernest Craddock 1892-1969, A Short Biography
          Privately produced, 1994